THE QUEEN

70 GLORIOUS YEARS

THE OFFICIAL PLATINUM JUBILEE SOUVENIR

EARLY LIFE

Princess Elizabeth and Dookie the corgi, 1936

———————

The Queen is known the world over for her fondness for animals, especially her affection for Pembroke Welsh corgis, originally bred by farmers for herding cattle. This picture of the future Queen Elizabeth II shows how that love began early in life. Seated in the garden of her London home, she is hugging Dookie, the family's first corgi, acquired by her parents, the Duke and Duchess of York, in 1933. When a second corgi, named Jane, came along in 1936, the two dogs bred and two puppies were retained from the litter, and so the collection grew. The Princess was given another corgi, Susan, for her 18th birthday in 1944, and until recently all The Queen's corgis have been direct descendants from her – 14 generations in all.

Little did the Princess know at the time this charming photograph was taken that events would soon thrust her into the limelight. Born on 21 April 1926, the first child of the Duke of York, second son of King George V, and Lady Elizabeth Bowes-Lyon, she was third in line of succession to the throne. Her uncle, the Duke of York's older brother, succeeded to the throne as King Edward VIII on 20 January 1936, but abdicated on 10 December to marry Wallis Simpson. When her father, George VI, became King on 11 December 1936, Princess Elizabeth became heir presumptive to the throne.

Queen Elizabeth with Princess Elizabeth, 12 May 1937

Princess Elizabeth's father was crowned King George VI on 12 May 1937, the date that had previously been fixed for King Edward VIII's Coronation, an occasion full of splendour and ceremony that was attended by his two daughters, Princess Elizabeth, the future Queen Elizabeth II, and her younger sister, Princess Margaret.

Princess Elizabeth wrote a full account of the Coronation in a lined exercise book, which she dedicated 'To Mummy and Papa In Memory of Their Coronation From Lilibet [her family nickname] By Herself'. She described the service as '<u>very</u>, <u>very</u> wonderful', especially the moment when her mother was crowned and 'all the peeresses put on their coronets', although she did admit that 'the service got rather boring' at the end as 'it was all prayers' and 'we were all shivering because there was a most awful draught'.

She described the journey back to Buckingham Palace from Westminster Abbey and then the moment when 'we all went on to the balcony where <u>millions</u> of people were waiting below'.

This picture shows Princess Elizabeth on the balcony with her mother, the newly crowned Queen Elizabeth, consort of King George VI. The Queen wears her Coronation crown, while the Princess wears a silver-gilt coronet, both made especially for the occasion.

Wartime broadcast, 13 October 1940

———————

Between 1922 and 1964, young people all over the UK would tune in eagerly to the BBC Home Service every day between 5pm and 6pm for *The Children's Hour*, presented for many years by Derek McCulloch, known as 'Uncle Mac', former head of children's broadcasting at the BBC. Listeners enjoyed a mix of poetry and music, news, sports and film reviews, serialised stories, history plays, quizzes and competitions – a version in miniature of BBC radio's broadcasts for adults.

Tuning in on Sunday 13 October 1940, young listeners and their parents were in for a surprise as the voice of the 14-year-old Princess Elizabeth came over the airwaves. School-age children were evacuated from cities across the UK from the day that the Second World War was declared, on 3 September 1939. Princess Elizabeth sympathised with the thousands who had had to leave their homes, 'and be separated from your fathers and mothers', adding that: 'my sister Margaret Rose and I feel so much for you as we know from experience what it means to be away from those we love most of all'.

She thanked 'the kind people who have welcomed you to their homes in the country', and those who had given 'a wartime home' to British Guest Children in Canada, Australia, New Zealand, South Africa and the United States of America. She praised the work of 'our gallant sailors, soldiers and airmen' and ended by reminding listeners that it was for the sake of the 'children of today' that they were fighting.

Princess Margaret then spoke to wish everyone goodnight before Princess Elizabeth concluded with: 'goodnight, and good luck to you all'. Thus ended her first public speech, and the first of many occasions on which she gave a morale-boosting address to the nation. Eighty years later, on 5 April 2020, at the start of the global Covid-19 pandemic, The Queen made reference again to that first broadcast when she said: 'today, once again, many [people] will feel a painful sense of separation from their loved ones'.

This photograph of the 20-year-old Princess Elizabeth conversing with her father, King George VI, in the gardens at Royal Lodge in Windsor Great Park, was taken on a fine summer's day a little more than a year after the war had ended. The photograph was one from a series designed to break away from the more traditional formal and aloof style of royal portraiture and shows Princess Elizabeth and other members of the Royal Family in relatively relaxed poses.

The photographers – husband and wife team Lisa and Jimmy Sheridan, known as Studio Lisa – excelled at taking pictures of children and dogs. Having seen examples of their work, Princess Elizabeth's parents first invited them to take photographs of the family and their pets in 1936. This proved to be the start of a 30-year relationship during which Studio Lisa photographed three generations of the Windsor family.

Reminiscing about the many occasions on which she had photographed the Royal Family at Windsor during the war and afterwards, Lisa Sheridan (1894–1966) said that there was a clear bond of understanding between the King and Princess Elizabeth and that he made a point of explaining everything to her as a kindly father to his attentive young daughter and as present monarch to future queen.

Princess Elizabeth and Lieutenant Philip Mountbatten on the announcement
of their engagement, Buckingham Palace, 10 July 1947

———————

The 18-year-old Prince Philip of Greece and Denmark had been enrolled
at the Royal Naval College, Dartmouth, in May 1939 as a Special Entry
Cadet. When King George VI visited the College to undertake an inspection,
Prince Philip was asked to entertain his third cousins, Princess Elizabeth,
then aged 13, and her sister Princess Margaret, then aged nine. The cousins
kept in touch and Philip became a regular guest at Buckingham Palace
and Windsor Castle, joining the family's Christmas celebrations, including
pantomime performances, dancing and games of charades.

Philip joined the Royal Family for their summer visit to Balmoral Castle
in 1946 and a year later, on 9 July 1947, the Court Circular declared: 'It is
with the greatest pleasure that The King and Queen announce the betrothal
of their dearly beloved daughter The Princess Elizabeth to Lieutenant Philip
Mountbatten, R.N., son of the late Prince Andrew of Greece and Princess
Andrew (Princess Alice of Battenberg), to which union The King has gladly
given his consent.'

Lieutenant Mountbatten himself designed the ring that he gave to
Princess Elizabeth to mark their engagement: made from platinum, it was
set with diamonds from a tiara that had once belonged to his mother.

Princess Elizabeth and the infant Prince Charles, December 1948

———————————

On 14 November 1948, Royal Household staff attached a handwritten notice to the railings at Buckingham Palace announcing that 'The Princess Elizabeth, Duchess of Edinburgh, was safely delivered of a Prince at nine fourteen pm today. Her Royal Highness and her son are both doing well.' The announcement was signed by the four doctors who attended the birth.

The King and Queen gave their daughter a brooch to celebrate the new arrival, in the form of a jewel-encrusted basket of flowers. Princess Elizabeth chose to wear that brooch for this official portrait, taken by Cecil Beaton (1904–80) a month after the birth. Swaddled in the lace of the cradle, which frames the radiantly lit face of Princess Elizabeth, Prince Charles looks out towards us as if aware of his destiny. Cecil Beaton recorded in his diary that the Prince 'interrupted a long, contented sleep to do my bidding and open his blue eyes to stare long and wonderingly into the camera lens, the beginning of a lifetime in the glare of public duty'.

As well as choosing it for this, Prince Charles's first official portrait, The Queen wore the basket of flowers brooch in 2013 at the christening of her great-grandson, Prince George (page 122). She also wore it for her Christmas broadcast in 2013, sitting in front of a picture of that christening and one of her late father, King George VI.

Dancing at the Hotel Phoenicia, Malta, 3 December 1949

After his marriage to Princess Elizabeth on 20 November 1947, Prince Philip returned to naval duties and in 1949 he was appointed second-in-command of the destroyer HMS *Chequers*, part of the Mediterranean fleet stationed in Malta. For the next two years, Princess Elizabeth divided her time between Britain and Malta.

On 20 November the Princess joined Prince Philip for their second wedding anniversary, and she spent her first Christmas on the island as the guest of the Earl and Countess Mountbatten of Burma, Prince Philip's uncle and aunt, at the Villa Guardamangia, in Pietà. While she was there she unveiled new panels at the base of the War Memorial in Floriana commemorating the Maltese who lost their lives in the two World Wars. She attended a gymkhana and watched the Duke play polo. Before she left the island on 26 December 1949 she and the Duke of Edinburgh attended the Christmas ball of the island's Saddle Club, where they joined enthusiastically in an eightsome reel, a popular Scottish dance.

In July 1951 the couple left Malta for good as Princess Elizabeth took on more of her father's public duties.

The Queen returns to London from Kenya, 7 February 1952

In February 1952, Princess Elizabeth and Prince Philip were enjoying a brief break from royal duties, having just completed a major tour together of Canada and the United States of America. They planned to undertake a long-arranged tour of Commonwealth nations, including Ceylon (now Sri Lanka), Australia and New Zealand in place of the King, whose recent surgery meant he was unable to travel.

Sadly the King passed away in his sleep on the night of 5/6 February at the age of 56. It was in Kenya, at the Sagana Lodge, to which the royal couple had just returned, having spent the previous night in a treetop cabin surrounded by wild animals at the Treetops Hotel, that Princess Elizabeth was given the news of her father's death. The planned tour was immediately cancelled and arrangements were quickly put in place for the couple to return to London where the new Queen was greeted on arrival on 7 February by Prime Minister Winston Churchill, Leader of the Opposition Clement Attlee, Foreign Secretary Anthony Eden and Lord President of the Council, Lord Woolton.

The following day, Princess Elizabeth was formally proclaimed Queen, Head of the Commonwealth and Defender of the Faith at a ceremony in St James's Palace before 150 Lords of the Council, Commonwealth representatives and City of London officials. Responding to the official proclamation, Queen Elizabeth II said: 'by the sudden death of my dear father I am called to assume the duties and responsibilities of sovereignty. My heart is too full for me to say more to you today than I shall always work, as my father did throughout his reign, to advance the happiness and prosperity of my peoples, spread as they are all the world over.'

The Queen arrives for her Coronation, 2 June 1953

Accompanied by Prince Philip (wearing full dress naval uniform) and attended by six Maids of Honour, The Queen arrived at Westminster Abbey on the day of her Coronation, 2 June 1953, in the Gold State Coach, first used for the State Opening of Parliament by George III in 1762, and used to convey the Sovereign to all Coronations since that of George IV in 1821.

When it became known that the Coronation would be televised, TV sales and rentals boomed. It is estimated that 27 million people in the UK watched the BBC broadcast out of a population of 36 million, the first time many of them had ever seen a televised event and the first time in history that people other than the monarch's close associates had witnessed a coronation.

Before, during and after the Coronation ceremony, The Queen wore several different garments. She arrived at Westminster Abbey wearing the Coronation Dress seen in this photograph. Designed by Norman Hartnell (1901–79), the dress is encrusted with seed pearls and crystals to create a glittering lattice-work effect. The exquisite embroidery in gold and silver thread and pastel-coloured silks incorporates garlands of flowers emblematic of the nations of the United Kingdom and the Commonwealth. Over this, The Queen wore a long mantle of crimson velvet, known as the Robe of State, which she continues to wear for the State Opening of Parliament.

On leaving the Abbey after her Coronation, The Queen wore the Robe of Estate, a magnificent robe of purple velvet with gold embroidery, created especially for the occasion, decorated with the royal cipher (EIIR) and a border of olive branches and wheat ears, symbolising peace and prosperity. Measuring more than 6.5 metres in length, from the shoulder to the tip of the train, the robe was commissioned from Ede & Ravenscroft, the long-established firm of tailors and robe makers, and the embroidery was completed by a team of twelve embroideresses working together at the Royal School of Needlework for a total of 3,500 hours.

ICONIC PORTRAITS

HM Queen Elizabeth II, 15 April 1952

One of the first duties of the young Queen following her accession was to sit for an official photograph for use on the UK's postage stamps. Dorothy Wilding (1893–1976) took 59 photographs on 26 February 1952 showing The Queen dressed in a variety of gowns designed by Norman Hartnell and wearing various royal accessories. The favoured image showed The Queen wearing the Diamond Diadem but looking to the right, so a second sitting was arranged for 15 April 1952, resulting in this photograph showing The Queen facing to the left, as was normal for postage stamps.

This and other photographs from the second sitting served as the basis for the image used on all the UK's postage stamps between 1953 and 1971, as well as providing the official portrait of The Queen that was sent to every British embassy throughout the world. The first stamps to include the portrait were issued on 3 June 1953 to celebrate the Coronation. Printed at twice the size of previously issued definitive stamps, the various designs incorporate Coronation regalia, the daffodil, rose, thistle and shamrock symbols of the four UK nations and The Queen in coronation robes wearing St Edward's Crown and holding the Sovereign's orb and sceptre.

HM Queen Elizabeth II on Coronation Day, 2 June 1953

Cecil Beaton was chosen to take the official photographs for the Coronation, and he used the Green Drawing Room at Buckingham Palace as the location. He employed a variety of theatrical backdrops depicting the interior and exterior of Westminster Abbey, framed by velvet curtains, for the pictures that he took of The Queen on her own, with the Duke of Edinburgh and with various other members of the Royal Family, including the Queen Mother and the young Prince Charles and Princess Anne.

In this portrait, The Queen is seated on a gilded armchair, wearing the Imperial State Crown against a backdrop of the magnificent Henry VII Lady Chapel in Westminster Abbey. She holds the Sovereign's sceptre tipped with a diamond-encrusted cross in her right hand and the golden orb in her left. She is wearing the embroidered and beaded Coronation Dress designed by Norman Hartnell, and the purple velvet Coronation Robe of Estate edged with ermine.

The photograph to the left shows Cecil Beaton and his two assistants (John Drysdale and Ray Harwood) taking the photographs, which appeared in publications around the world, serving as an indelible reminder of that historic day.

The Queen on board HMY Britannia, March 1972

Her Majesty's Yacht *Britannia* was built by the Clydebank shipyard company John Brown & Co. Ltd, and launched by The Queen on 16 April 1953. For the next 44 years, *Britannia* served as an ocean-going royal residence, enabling The Queen to make more than 700 overseas visits and to entertain world leaders and other guests all over the globe. It was also the setting for family holidays: The Queen once described the yacht as 'the one place where I can truly relax'.

In this informal photograph, The Queen leans on the rail of the upper deck of HMY *Britannia* enjoying the sight of a bedraggled Patrick Lichfield being 'ducked' in a temporary swimming pool erected on deck as part of an initiation rite to commemorate his first crossing of the Equator.

Patrick Lichfield, 5th Earl of Lichfield (1939–2005), had been invited to join the royal party on The Queen's Far Eastern tour to take photographs to mark the Silver Wedding anniversary of The Queen and Prince Philip in November 1972. Lichfield later wrote that he had been aware that the ritual was about to take place and 'I had the wit to take a waterproof camera with me and when I came up for about the third time, I took a picture of The Queen up on the bridge laughing at me'.

The Queen arriving at Aberdeen Airport, 22 June 1974

Every summer, The Queen travels to Balmoral Castle, the Scottish home of the Royal Family since it was purchased by Prince Albert in 1852 as a gift for Queen Victoria. Here The Queen is able to immerse herself in the beautiful river, mountain and coastal scenery of Royal Deeside, in Aberdeenshire, relaxing with her family and enjoying country walks around the Balmoral estate with her beloved corgis.

Three corgis accompanied The Queen when she disembarked from the aeroplane at Aberdeen airport ahead of her holiday in 1974 dressed in a forest green skirt suit with pearls and a black handbag. This now famous image, taken by Anwar Hussein (born 1938), the Tanzanian photo-journalist, featured in the exhibition *The Queen: 60 Photographs for 60 Years*, mounted first at Windsor Castle and then the Palace of Holyroodhouse in 2012 on the occasion of her Diamond Jubilee, marking 60 years on the throne.

HM Queen Elizabeth II, 1968

The photographs of The Queen taken by Cecil Beaton were influential in shaping the image of the monarch over three decades, marking significant events in her life, such as the birth of Prince Charles (page 14) and the Coronation (page 24). This was the last photograph Beaton took of Elizabeth II, although he continued to photograph other members of the Royal Family until 1979.

The occasion for this strikingly simple image was a forthcoming exhibition of Beaton's work that opened at the National Portrait Gallery on 1 November 1968. Beaton was inspired by Pietro Annigoni's celebrated portrait of The Queen, commissioned by the City of London livery company, the Worshipful Company of Fishmongers, and completed in 1955. In that painting, The Queen was portrayed in the robes of the Order of the Garter, but Beaton chose a much plainer Admiral's Boat Cloak for his photograph.

Beaton's photographic archive was bequeathed to the Victoria and Albert Museum in London, whose catalogue describes this as 'a contemplative and timeless image of the monarch', all the more powerful for its simplicity, without the distractions of jewels, costumes and regalia.

Lucian Freud painting The Queen's portrait, 2001

David Dawson (born 1960) took a series of photographs to document the work of the highly regarded figurative artist Lucian Freud (1922–2011). This picture was taken by Dawson in 2001 in the conservation studio at St James's Palace where The Queen sat on a number of occasions for the portrait that Freud presented to the monarch 'as soon as the paint had dried' to mark her Golden Jubilee in 2002.

The head and shoulders view of The Queen, wearing the Diamond Diadem, provoked mixed reactions. Some critics thought it unflattering, but Charles Saumarez Smith, Director of the National Portrait Gallery at the time, hailed it as 'a thought-provoking and psychologically penetrating contribution to royal iconography'. He went on to say that it 'breaks the mould of royal portraits which tend to be commissioned from highly traditional artists'.

The Queen wearing Garter Robes, 28 March 2007

The renowned American portrait photographer Annie Leibovitz (born 1949) is the most recent of a long tradition of female photographers favoured by the Royal Family, following in the footsteps of Lisa Sheridan (page 10) and Dorothy Wilding (page 22). In 2007 she was commissioned to take a series of photographs of The Queen ahead of the State Visit to the United States of America that took place between 3 and 8 May that year. With only limited time to do her work, Leibovitz used the natural light from the window in the White Drawing Room at Buckingham Palace to illuminate The Queen, who is wearing the mantle of the Order of the Garter.

Later that year the BBC showed a promotional trailer for its documentary film, *A Year with The Queen*, in which the misleading impression was given that The Queen was angered by some of Leibovitz's suggestions for how she should dress, for which the BBC subsequently apologised. Leibovitz was later invited to take the photographs at Windsor Castle to mark Her Majesty's 90th birthday in 2016, showing her walking with her dogs in the private grounds of Windsor Castle and surrounded by seven of her grandchildren and great-grandchildren in the Green Drawing Room (page 124).

The Queen's sense of humour is to the fore in this selfie taken by Jayde Taylor of herself and fellow Australian hockey player Brooke Peris at the 2014 Commonwealth Games, held between 23 July and 3 August in Glasgow. The photograph, which appeared on the front page of newspapers around the world, seems to show The Queen intruding into the picture – a tactic known as 'photobombing'. Jayde subsequently admitted that they timed the shot, knowing Her Majesty was moving into view, but the resulting image was retweeted millions of times around the world and brought fame to the two young hockey players. Both of them went on to score a goal each for the Australian women's team, which won the gold medal (with 16 points) after knocking England into second place (11 points).

Formally opening the 2014 Games the previous day, The Queen referred to the 'shared ideals and ambitions' that bind the nations and territories of the Commonwealth into a 'diverse, resourceful and cohesive family'. She also reminded everyone that young people under 25 years of age made up half of all Commonwealth citizens. 'It is to you', she said, 'that we entrust our values and our future.'

The Queen on tour, 11 December 1953

As well as being the subject of hundreds of official photographs and millions of pictures taken by press photographers and well-wishers around the world, The Queen has, on occasion, kept her own photographic record of the events that she has witnessed. She was given her first camera, a Kodak Box Brownie, by her father, King George VI, in the 1930s. This photograph shows the newly crowned Queen on board SS *Gothic* wielding a cine-camera to record the firing of a 21-gun royal salute from HMS *Sheffield* when handing over the duty of escorting SS *Gothic* to the New Zealand light cruiser HMNZS *Black Prince* on 11 December 1953.

The Queen and the Duke of Edinburgh set sail on SS *Gothic* on a six-month tour of the Commonwealth in November 1953, visiting first Bermuda, Jamaica, Fiji and Tonga before arriving in New Zealand on 23 December; from there the royal couple visited Australia, the Cocos (Keeling) Islands, Ceylon (now Sri Lanka), Aden, Uganda, Malta and Gibraltar, returning to the United Kingdom in May 1954.

After completing its escort duty, HMS *Sheffield* returned to Panama and to duties in the Caribbean, where she served as the flagship of the 8th Cruiser Squadron before eventually being broken up in 1967 (her battle ensign and bell, made in Sheffield, today hang in Sheffield Cathedral). *Black Prince*, originally commissioned by the Royal Navy in 1943, was officially transferred to the Royal New Zealand Navy in 1946 and carried out Royal Tour escort duties from December 1953 after a major refit. She was eventually sold to Japan and broken up in 1962. After serving as the royal yacht between 1952 and 1954, SS *Gothic* returned to regular duties as a passenger and cargo liner, sailing between London and New Zealand. She was finally broken up for scrap in 1969.

THE ROLE OF THE MONARCH

Maundy Service, 10 April 1952

———————

In her first public engagement since the funeral of her father on 15 February, The Queen, flanked by Yeomen of the Guard and accompanied by the Dean, took part in the Maundy Thursday service at Westminster Abbey on 10 April 1952. As part of the service, The Queen distributed special Maundy Money coins to deserving citizens.

According to the Gospels, on the day before his Crucifixion, Jesus washed the feet of his disciples as an act of love and humility and commanded his followers to do the same: the word Maundy derives from the Latin word *mandatum*, meaning 'command'. Medieval monarchs continued the foot-washing tradition, which in time changed to the distribution of food, clothing and shoes to the poor and eventually to the gift of money.

The recipients are selected in recognition of their services to the Church and to the local community. The number of male and female recipients each year is equal to the monarch's age, and they receive two purses from The Queen: the red purse contains a small sum of money in ordinary coinage in lieu of food and clothing and the white purse contains specially minted silver coins amounting to the same number of pence as the years of the Sovereign's age.

The Queen has kept up the custom throughout her reign, choosing a different cathedral, abbey, minster or royal chapel for the ceremony every year, though Covid-19 restrictions prevented her from doing so in person in 2020 and 2021, and purses were distributed by post instead.

The Queen at her desk, 1969

Seated at her desk in Buckingham Palace, The Queen is seen opening one of the red despatch boxes that she has dealt with on most days of her reign, the exceptions being The Queen's official days off: Christmas Day and Easter Sunday.

The use of boxes bound in red leather dates back to the reign of Elizabeth I, when such boxes were used to deliver important messages for her attention. Today (see page 136) they contain documents and papers selected for The Queen's attention by the Private Secretary, the senior operational member of the Royal Household. These include matters requiring the monarch's assent or her signature: The Queen continues to sign all legislation passed by Parliament. Along with briefing papers for forthcoming meetings and documents from the Government, Parliament and Commonwealth, there might also be honours to approve and correspondence to sign.

Just as the red despatch box used by the Chancellor of the Exchequer has become a well-recognised symbol of Budget Day, The Queen's despatch box has become synonymous with her constitutional role as Head of State, in which she has the right 'to be consulted, to encourage and to warn' her Ministers.

President Kennedy visits Buckingham Palace, 5 June 1961

Two of the world's most glamorous couples were photographed together at Buckingham Palace on 5 June 1961, when the US President, John F. Kennedy, and his wife, Jacqueline Kennedy, were guests at a dinner party hosted by The Queen and the Duke of Edinburgh in their honour. The President and Mrs Kennedy had come to London on a private visit, for the christening of Mrs Kennedy's niece, Anna Christina, daughter of Jacqueline's younger sister Lee, wife of Prince Stanislas Radziwiłł of Poland.

As well as acting as godfather to Anna Christina, President Kennedy took the opportunity to visit Prime Minister Harold Macmillan at 10 Downing Street to discuss relations with Russia. Mr Macmillan was also a guest at the dinner, which he described in his diary as a 'very pleasant' evening.

The Queen and Mrs Kennedy both lived up to their reputation as style icons of the day, The Queen with her new shorter hairstyle wearing a light blue Norman Hartnell A-line dress of tulle, while the First Lady dressed for dinner in an ice blue silk gown designed by the New York couturier Chez Ninon.

Jacqueline Kennedy visited The Queen again the following year, while staying in London with her sister. The Queen invited the First Lady to lunch on 28 March 1962. Mrs Kennedy told the press later 'how grateful I am and how charming she was'. In 1965, two years after the assassination of John F. Kennedy, The Queen unveiled a memorial to the late President at Runnymede, Berkshire, at a ceremony attended by Jacqueline Kennedy, along with her children Caroline and John.

_____

Cementing the special relationship between the UK and the USA, The Queen has played host to eleven US Presidents during her reign, from President Eisenhower (in 1959) to President Biden (2021). President Obama and his wife Michelle made their first State Visit between 23 and 26 May 2011. They were welcomed to Buckingham Palace with a 41-gun salute and gifts were then exchanged. The Obamas presented The Queen with a leather-bound album of memorabilia and photographs from her parents' 1939 visit to the USA, while The Queen presented facsimiles of letters from the Royal Archives exchanged between past US presidents and Queen Victoria.

At the State Banquet, The Queen proposed a toast to 'the tried, tested, and, yes, special relationship between our two countries [and] to the continued health, happiness, and prosperity of the people of the United States of America, and especially to the health of President and Mrs Obama'.

President Obama responded with a toast to the 'vitality of the special relationship between our peoples', based on 'the rock-solid foundation built during Queen Elizabeth's lifetime of extraordinary service to her nation and to the world'. He also added warm greetings from his daughters Malia and Sasha, 'who adored you even before you let them ride on a carriage on the palace grounds'.

Presenting ambassadorial Credentials, 16 March 2010

In this photograph, His Excellency the Ambassador Mr Werner Matias Romero of El Salvador presents his Credentials to The Queen at Buckingham Palace. At any one time, London has more than 170 Ambassadors and High Commissioners in residence, and each one of them has an Audience with The Queen shortly after taking up their role.

Ambassadors and High Commissioners represent the interests of their country in the UK by building diplomatic ties, the only difference being in their titles: High Commissioners come from Commonwealth countries and Ambassadors do not.

Diplomatic Audiences have barely changed since Victorian times and involve some uniquely royal touches. Diplomats are collected from their Embassy or residence in a State Landau (a ceremonial horse-drawn carriage). They are led to Buckingham Palace by a second carriage – that of the Marshal of the Diplomatic Corps, the member of the Royal Household responsible for The Queen's links with the London diplomatic community.

At the start of the Audience, diplomats present their Letters of Credence (for Ambassadors) or Letters of High Commission (for High Commissioners). This is a formal letter from the diplomat's Head of State to The Queen asking her to give 'credence' to the new Ambassador or High Commissioner – hence the letters are often termed 'Credentials'. The word is derived from the Latin *credere*, 'to believe', and it says in effect that Her Majesty can take it on trust that the appointed diplomat has the authority to speak on behalf of their country.

Garter Day, 15 June 2009

Edward III (1312–77) founded the Order of the Garter in 1348 as a way of rewarding those supporters who did most to help him in battle and further the cause of the king's claim to the French throne. Membership remains a mark of royal favour and is limited to 24 Knights Companion, in addition to The Queen (the Sovereign of the Garter) and the Prince of Wales (the Royal Knight Companion of the Garter).

The origins of the Garter insignia and the motto of the Order – *Honi soit qui mal y pense* ('Shame on him who thinks evil of it') – are lost in the mists of time, but there is no doubting the pride with which the Garter is worn by members of the UK's most senior order of chivalry, appointed in recognition of their contribution to national life or their service to the Sovereign. The Queen appointed the first Ladies Companion of the Garter in 1987.

New appointments to the Order are announced on St George's Day (23 April) but Garter Day, with its colourful pageantry and installation ceremony, takes place in June, when members of the Royal Family join the Sovereign and the other members of the Order at a service in the Order's spiritual home, St George's Chapel, Windsor.

Members of the Order wear black velvet hats with white plumes and blue velvet robes with the badge of the Order – the Cross of St George within the Garter surrounded by radiating silver beams – on the left shoulder. They are accompanied by the Constable and Governor of Windsor Castle, the Military Knights of Windsor and various Officers of Arms in their colourful tabards and dress uniforms.

Inspecting the Coldstream Guards, 22 June 1964

As Sovereign, The Queen is Head of the Armed Services in the United Kingdom. George II was the last British monarch to lead their army in battle – at the Battle of Dettingen in 1743 during the War of the Austrian Succession – but it is a tradition of very long standing that members of the Royal Family serve in the forces, and several of The Queen's children and grandchildren have done so.

The Duke of Edinburgh saw active service during the Second World War during the Battle of Cape Matapan (27–29 March 1941) and in the Allied invasion of Sicily, codenamed Operation Husky, from 9 July to 17 August 1943. The Queen herself was the first female member of the Royal Family to join the Armed Services as a full-time active member when, as Princess Elizabeth, she joined the Auxiliary Territorial Service (ATS) as a Subaltern (junior officer) in 1945 (page 98). It was during her time in the ATS that The Queen learnt to drive and to maintain vehicles.

The monarch has a particular relationship with the Coldstream Guards – shown here being inspected by The Queen on 22 June 1964 at Windsor Castle – because of their role as part of the Household Division, one of whose principal roles is the protection of the Sovereign, their Colonel-in-Chief – hence the duties they perform at the various royal palaces, including the ceremony of Changing the Guard. Formed in 1650, they are the Army's oldest continuously serving regiment.

Trooping the Colour, 13 June 1981

———————————

The Coldstream Guards play an important role in the colourful display of military precision, horsemanship and music known as Trooping the Colour that has marked the Sovereign's official birthday since 1748. The ceremony has its origins in the practice of parading a regiment's colours, or flag, in front of the troops so that they would recognise and follow the flag in battle, the flag itself being the symbol of the monarch and of the regiment's honour – the loss of the flag in battle meant confusion and possible defeat.

More than 1,400 soldiers, 200 horses and 400 musicians take part in the parade as it travels from Buckingham Palace to Horse Guard's Parade, accompanied by The Queen, who used to attend on horseback herself but now travels by carriage. The Queen is greeted by a Royal salute and carries out an inspection of the troops, who wear their ceremonial uniform of red tunics and bearskin hats. After the military bands have performed, the escorted Regimental Colour, or flag, is processed down the ranks of soldiers. The Queen then leads the soldiers back to Buckingham Palace, and the display closes with an RAF fly-past, watched by members of the Royal Family from the balcony at Buckingham Palace, while a 41-gun salute is fired in Green Park.

Garden Party at the Palace of Holyroodhouse, 3 July 2019

Every summer, The Queen invites more than 30,000 people to Garden
Parties held in the grounds of Buckingham Palace and (as shown in
this picture) at the Palace of Holyroodhouse in Edinburgh. This is an
opportunity for The Queen and other members of the Royal Family
to meet a broad range of people from all walks of life, all of whom have
made a positive impact on their community. Guests in turn have the
opportunity to enjoy the gardens at both palaces. Typically, there are
four Garden Parties a year (three at Buckingham Palace and one at
Holyroodhouse), and on each occasion, guests consume 27,000 cups
of tea, 20,000 sandwiches and 20,000 slices of cakes.

Garden Parties have been held at Buckingham Palace since the
1860s when they formed one of the events of the London social season
that was enjoyed exclusively by the landed gentry and the aristocracy.
The Queen's father, King George VI, began the move to a more inclusive
event when he used Garden Parties as an opportunity to thank members
of the armed forces for their service during the Second World War.

The Garden Party at Holyroodhouse is one of the events that form
part of the annual Holyrood Week, known in Scotland as Royal Week,
when The Queen is welcomed to the city of Edinburgh by the Lord
Provost who offers her the symbolic keys to the city. The Queen gives
the keys back with the words: 'I return these keys, being perfectly
convinced that they cannot be placed in better hands than those of
the Lord Provost and Councillors of my good City of Edinburgh'.
During Holyrood Week The Queen undertakes a number of official
engagements and visits various parts of Scotland for events that
celebrate Scottish culture, history and achievement.

Tower of London, 16 October 2014

One of The Queen's most important duties is to lead the nation in remembrance of those millions of people around the world who sacrificed their lives during two World Wars and subsequent conflicts. In 2014, the 100th anniversary of the outbreak of the First World War was marked at the Tower of London by an art installation which saw the moat filled with 888,246 ceramic red poppies, each one representing a member of the British or Commonwealth armed forces killed in the service of their country.

The work's title – 'Blood Swept Lands and Seas of Red' – was taken from the first line of a poem by an unknown soldier who died on the Western Front. Paul Cummins, the creator of the installation, found the poem while undertaking research in the Chesterfield Local Studies Library, in Derbyshire.

The Queen visited the Tower to meet Paul Cummins and see the memorial display on 16 October 2014. She also laid her own poppy wreath as a tribute to those who made the ultimate sacrifice. A team of some 17,500 volunteers from across the UK helped to place the poppies in the moat under the direction of stage designer Tom Piper, the last poppy being planted on Remembrance Day, 11 November 2014, by Harry Hayes, a 13-year-old cadet from the Combined Cadet Force. Five million people from countries around the world travelled to the Tower of London to see the poppies, which were subsequently sold to raise money for six service charities.

Christmas Day broadcast, 25 December 1957

For millions of people around the world, The Queen's Christmas broadcast is as important a part of the day as Christmas pudding and the exchange of presents. The first broadcast was delivered by King George V in 1932 by radio. The Queen's address on 25 December 1957, 25 years later, has gone down in history because it was the first to be televised. As The Queen said at the beginning of her broadcast, 'I very much hope that this new medium will make my Christmas message more personal and direct'.

The personal nature of the Christmas Day broadcast is one of its characteristics. This is an occasion when The Queen shares her thoughts on a topic of her own choosing, without being advised by the Government. In 1957, wearing a seasonal dress of gold lamé, she took as her subject the Commonwealth of Nations, one of the abiding themes of her reign.

An early version of the Commonwealth had been formed in 1926 and this was given fresh impetus in the years following the Second World War when many nations that were once part of the British Empire became self-governing, leading to the formation of the modern Commonwealth of Nations in 1949 (see page 86). The Queen referred to the speed with which these changes were taking place and the sense of bewilderment that many might feel as a result, but she urged everyone to take 'pride in the new Commonwealth we are building' and 'work together as friends'.

Seated in the Long Library at her Sandringham home, at the desk used by her father and grandfather, she read the words of Mr Valiant-for-Truth from John Bunyan's work, *The Pilgrim's Progress*: 'though with great difficulty I am got hither, yet now I do not repent me of all the trouble I have been at to arrive where I am'.

TRAVELLING THE KINGDOM AND THE COMMONWEALTH

The Queen travels on Concorde, 2 November 1977

———————

The Queen is pictured here during her flight home from Bridgetown, Barbados, on completion of her Silver Jubilee tour of Canada and the Caribbean, undertaken between 14 and 31 October. This was The Queen's first flight on Concorde, the new Anglo-French-designed supersonic aircraft that had entered service in 1976 and operated for 27 years. Her Majesty is seen taking a close look at the crowded panels of instruments when she paid a visit to the flight deck of the pioneering aircraft.

Technological advances like Concorde that have taken place during The Queen's 70-year reign have enabled her to become the most travelled monarch in history. In the course of a busy travel schedule she has visited every part of the United Kingdom, from Shetland to the Isles of Scilly, to participate in civic and community events, from the opening of new buildings to acts of commemoration and celebration.

The Queen and other members of the Royal Family carry out more than 2,000 engagements each year, travelling by road, rail, sea and air. The Royal Train is fitted out with catering and office facilities to allow The Queen to work while travelling. Aeroplanes and helicopters are also used by the Royal Family for travelling to engagements, and these are all painted in the same distinctive burgundy livery, as is the fleet of royal cars.

As Head of the Commonwealth, The Queen has personally reinforced the links between the 54 member states through more than 200 royal tours, visiting every Commonwealth country at least once with the exception of Cameroon, which joined in 1995, and Rwanda, which joined in 2009. The Queen undertakes additional tours with advice from her Government. Once a tour has been agreed, an official invitation is sent by the Head of State of the host country to The Queen, who sends a personal reply. Her Majesty is closely involved in the planning of the itinerary.

The Queen visits Caernarfon Castle, Wales, 27 April 2010

In 2010 The Queen and the Duke of Edinburgh visited Caernarfon during a two-day tour of Wales. Hundreds of children waved Welsh flags and cheered as the couple made their way through the grounds of Caernarfon Castle, which had been the site of the investiture of The Prince of Wales more than 40 years before (page 112).

The Queen's connection with Wales dates from her childhood. As a sixth birthday present, the people of Wales presented Princess Elizabeth with a Wendy house, called 'Y Bwythyn Bach' (the Little Cottage). This traditional thatched cottage still sits in the grounds of Royal Lodge, The Queen's childhood residence near Windsor Castle, and has since been enjoyed by generations of royal children. Also of Welsh origin is The Queen's wedding ring which, like that of her parents, Lady Elizabeth Bowes-Lyon and the Duke of York (later Queen Elizabeth and King George VI), is made from gold from the Clogau St David's mine near Dolgellau, in Snowdonia.

In a speech to the National Assembly for Wales (now the Senedd Cymru) in Cardiff at the end of her three-day Golden Jubilee tour in June 2002, The Queen said: 'I follow with great interest the work of all the parliaments and assemblies of the United Kingdom. I hope and pray that you, as members of the National Assembly for Wales, will continue to work together to serve the common good and the people of this proud and beautiful land.'

The Queen on a walkabout in Perth, Scotland, 19 May 1977

Since the 1970s, 'walkabouts' have been an important part of any royal visit. Her Majesty pioneered the tradition during her first walkabout on the tour of Australia and New Zealand in the spring of 1970. The practice was established to allow The Queen and other members of the Royal Family to meet as many well-wishers as possible, not just officials and dignitaries. Walkabouts remain a mainstay of royal visits and tours today, in all weathers!

On this walkabout during a Silver Jubilee visit to Perth in May 1977 The Queen was greeted by crowds waving the red and gold Scottish Standard, The Queen's official banner in Scotland, also known as the 'Lion Rampant'. When she is not in residence, this flag also flies at Her Majesty's official residence in Scotland, the Palace of Holyroodhouse in Edinburgh, and at her private home, Balmoral Castle in Aberdeenshire. When she is in residence, the Royal Standard is flown.

Returning to Perth with Prince Philip for the Diamond Jubilee tour in 2012, The Queen spoke of her personal connection to Scotland, which, she said, 'has played such a very special part in our lives, and that of my family, over the years … we have greatly enjoyed our frequent visits'.

The Queen and the Duke of Edinburgh visit Belfast, Northern Ireland, 27 June 2012

The Queen has visited Northern Ireland 25 times since 1949. In 2002, during a visit to Stormont, the seat of the Northern Ireland Assembly in Belfast, The Queen spoke of her affection for the people of the country: 'over the last half century, I have always enjoyed my visits to Northern Ireland. Even in the most troubled of times, I have been heartened by the warmth and good humour of the people I have met.'

As part of the Diamond Jubilee celebrations, marking the 60th anniversary of The Queen's accession, The Queen and Prince Philip visited Belfast again in 2012. This striking picture shows the royal couple riding through the crowds in a specially converted open-top vehicle, waving to the well-wishers who had gathered to greet them on the final day of their visit.

On 3 May 2021, The Queen sent a message to the people of Northern Ireland to mark the centenary of its foundation in 1921. The anniversary 'reminds us of our complex history', she said, adding that it provides 'an opportunity to reflect on our togetherness and our diversity'. She paid tribute to 'a generation of leaders who had the vision and courage to put reconciliation before division' and said that 'across generations, the people of Northern Ireland are choosing to build an inclusive, prosperous, and hopeful society, strengthened by the gains of the peace process. May this be our guiding thread in the coming years.'

The Queen meeting traders at the English Market in Cork on her State Visit to Ireland, 20 May 2011

In May 2011 The Queen made a historic State Visit to the Republic of Ireland – the first by a British monarch since the country's independence in 1922 – heralding a new era in relations between the United Kingdom and its close neighbour. The programme included a meeting with Taoiseach Enda Kenny at the Government Buildings in Dublin, and a State Dinner at Dublin Castle with Irish President Mary McAleese. In her speech at the State Dinner, Her Majesty declared: 'we celebrate together in the widespread spirit of goodwill and deep mutual understanding that has served to make the relationship more harmonious, close as good neighbours should always be'.

On the final day of her four-day tour, Her Majesty visited the renowned English Market in the city of Cork, so called since the mid-19th century to distinguish it from the nearby Irish Market. Here, amidst the recently restored splendour of the cast-iron columns and tiled fountain, the Queen met market traders and was photographed sharing a joke with fishmonger Pat O'Connell, who told her that the ugly monkfish was nicknamed 'the mother-in-law fish', adding that he had been very good friends with his own late mother-in-law.

*Adi Kainona presents The Queen with a bouquet of
Fijian flowers, Fiji, 17 December 1953*

———————

The 1953–4 tour of the Commonwealth was the first and longest tour
of Her Majesty's reign. Lasting seven months and encompassing the
Caribbean, Oceania, Asia and Africa, The Queen and the Duke of
Edinburgh travelled 40,000 miles between November 1953 and May
1954. At the beginning of The Queen's reign the Pacific Islands were
remote and difficult to visit, and for the most part could only be reached
by a journey involving several weeks at sea. In 1953 The Queen and
Prince Philip flew to the Caribbean, where they visited Bermuda on
24–25 November and Jamaica on 25–27 November before continuing
the tour by sea on SS *Gothic*, refitted to serve as a royal yacht (see page 38).

Arriving in Suva, the capital of Fiji, three weeks later, on 17 December,
Her Majesty welcomed the leading Fijian chiefs on board to perform
the greeting ceremony of *cavuikelekele*, as part of the formal invitation to
land. The paramount chief, Ratu Tevita Uluilakeba, then gave The Queen
a *tabua* (the polished tooth of a sperm whale), a mark of esteem and the
most prized possession of any Fijian ruler, which remains in the Royal
Collection today. The Queen was then greeted by Sir Ronald Garvey,
Governor of Fiji, and presented with a bouquet of Fijian flowers by
three-year-old Adi Kainona, daughter of Ratu Sir Penaia Ganilau, who
later served as the last Governor-General and first President of Fiji.

*The Queen riding on an elephant with the Maharaja of
Benares, India, 25 February 1961*

In 1961, The Queen paid her first visit to the Indian subcontinent on a
six-week tour of India, Pakistan and Nepal. During her visit to India,
The Queen travelled twice by elephant. First, on 23 January 1961, she made
a ceremonial entry into the heart of the City Palace in Jaipur, Rajasthan,
seated beside Sawai Man Singh II, the Maharaja of Jaipur. Shown here is her
subsequent visit to Benares (now Varanasi) on 25 February 1961, when she
rode through the city as a guest of the Maharaja, Vibhuti Narayan Singh,
on a 45-year-old elephant called Mangal Prasad, visiting Balua Ghat, on the
bank of the city's holy river, the Ganges.

After achieving independence in 1947, India was one of the first of a
number of nations whose new Presidents decided that they wished to become
part of the Commonwealth. Speaking at the State Banquet at Buckingham
Palace in 2009 during the State Visit of President Pratibha Patil, The Queen
said: 'relations between our two countries are built on strong and deep
foundations, and are set fair for the 21st century'.

The Queen visits Montserrat in the Caribbean, 19 February 1966

In February and March 1966 The Queen and Prince Philip undertook
a five-week tour of the Caribbean, visiting Guyana, Trinidad and Tobago,
Grenada, Saint Vincent, Barbados, Saint Lucia, Dominica, Antigua and
Barbuda, Saint Kitts and Nevis, The Bahamas and Jamaica. In a candid
snapshot taken during a one-day visit to Montserrat, one of the Leeward
Islands, Her Majesty is seen here smiling as she meets local school children
after attending the Harris Agricultural Show.

  The Queen's wardrobe is meticulously planned for each tour. The climate
must be considered, and the colours of the fabrics should allow The Queen
to be clearly visible among large crowds. Her Majesty's designers sometimes
select a fabric in the national colour of the host nation. Occasionally, emblems
particular to a region or country are incorporated into the design, usually
through embroidered decoration, as a way of paying a compliment to the
country being visited. Although not visible in this black-and-white photograph,
The Queen's dress and feathered hat were in an eye-catching bright yellow.

The Queen wearing a Maori cloak in New Zealand,
during the Silver Jubilee tour, 26 February 1977

During the 1953–4 Commonwealth tour, The Queen and Prince Philip
visited the Arawa Park racecourse in Rotorua, New Zealand. Here they
were presented with traditional Maori kiwi feather cloaks (*kahu kiwi*),
which are worn to symbolise chieftainship and high birth. The Queen
has worn her cloak on subsequent visits to the islands for local
anniversaries and events, including the commemoration in 1990 of
the 150th anniversary of the Treaty of Waitingi, New Zealand's
founding document, agreed between representatives of the British
Crown and a number of Maori chiefs on 6 February 1840.

This photograph of Her Majesty wearing the cloak was taken
in 1977, when she was welcomed by the Maori people in Gisborne,
on the North Island of New Zealand. The visit formed one stop on a
56,000-mile journey to 14 Commonwealth countries, undertaken to
celebrate the Silver Jubilee. It is estimated that three out of four New
Zealanders saw The Queen during her 1953 visit; the 1977 itinerary
was designed to follow closely that first itinerary so that the monarch
could meet as many people as possible.

New Zealand is a constitutional monarchy with The Queen as
Sovereign. As a constitutional monarch, The Queen of New Zealand
acts entirely on the advice of New Zealand Government Ministers, and
she is responsible for appointing a Governor-General for New Zealand,
which she does on the advice of the country's Prime Minister.

Mother Teresa is honoured by The Queen, 24 November 1983

In 1983, The Queen invested Mother Teresa of Calcutta as an honorary member of the Order of Merit at a ceremony at the Rashtrapati Bhavan, the official residence of the President of India. This historic meeting took place when Her Majesty was attending a meeting of the Commonwealth Heads of Government in New Delhi. In 2016 Mother Teresa was canonised for her work with the poor in India; that year The Queen quoted St Teresa in her televised Christmas broadcast: 'not all of us can do great things. But we can do small things with great love'.

The Order of Merit was founded by King Edward VII in 1902, and is in the sole gift of the Sovereign, recognising those who have rendered exceptional service. The Queen has only awarded the Order to recipients from Commonwealth countries on two other occasions: in 1963 to Sarvepalli Radhakrishnan, the second President of India, and in 1995 to Nelson Mandela, President of South Africa.

In the course of her reign The Queen has met figures who are considered seminal in the history of the modern world. Her meeting with the Chinese leader Deng Xiaoping in 1986 was seen as especially significant as she was the first reigning British monarch to visit the People's Republic of China. Three years later, on 7 April 1989, the first meeting for more than 20 years took place between a Soviet leader and a British monarch when President Mikhail Gorbachev of the USSR and his wife Raisa were entertained to lunch at Windsor Castle.

The Queen on a walkabout in South Africa, 22 March 1995

The Queen paid a historic visit to South Africa at the invitation of President Nelson Mandela in March 1995 – her first visit for 48 years and her first as Head of State. She had previously visited in 1947, accompanying her parents, King George VI and Queen Elizabeth, and her sister Princess Margaret on a three-month tour, during which she celebrated her 21st birthday in Cape Town. It was during this first visit that the Princess made an oath to the Commonwealth via radio broadcast: 'I declare before you all that my whole life whether it be long or short shall be devoted to your service and the service of our great imperial family to which we all belong.' The 1995 visit was particularly significant because it celebrated the return of South Africa to the Commonwealth after an absence of 32 years.

Here The Queen is seen meeting school children during a walkabout with Nceba Faku, who was elected the first Black mayor of the city of Port Elizabeth (now Gqeberha) in the country's first democratic local elections. The Queen recalled that visit to South Africa with Prince Philip when she spoke at the State Banquet held at Buckingham Palace on 3 March 2010 to welcome Jacob Zuma, President of South Africa, on a State Visit to the UK. 'We could see for ourselves how much the country had changed', she said. 'Just one year after the momentous elections which had brought President Mandela to power, a new atmosphere of self-confidence and positive hopes for the future was already very apparent.'

The Queen and the Duke of Edinburgh visit Canada, 17 May 2005

Canada is the country most visited by The Queen over the last 70 years. She has an important ceremonial and symbolic role as Queen of Canada, entirely separate from her role as Queen of the United Kingdom or any of her other realms. Represented in Canada by the Governor-General, The Queen is fully briefed by means of regular communications from her ministers and has face-to-face audiences with them where possible.

Since her first visit as Princess Elizabeth in 1951, she has often stated that Canada was a 'second home' where she felt herself at ease and enjoyed meeting Canadians from all walks of life and cultural groups, and exploring remote areas never previously visited by a reigning monarch.

Taken in 2005 during an eight-day State Visit to Saskatchewan and Alberta, this photograph depicts The Queen's delight as Prince Philip shows her a pair of moccasins that had been presented to him by the First Nations University of Canada in Regina. The Queen is seated between Montreal Lake Cree Chief Alphonse Bird and Dr Eber Hampton, President of the First Nations University of Canada. Some First Nations groups refer to the monarch as their grandmother and their special relationship goes back to her great-great-grandmother, Queen Victoria, who promised their community land rights, free education and health care.

The Queen celebrates the Diamond Anniversary
of the Commonwealth, Trinidad, 28 November 2009

In 2009 the Commonwealth of Nations celebrated its 60th anniversary. The Queen attended the 20th Commonwealth Heads of Government Meeting (CHOGM) in Trinidad and Tobago that November, declaring in her opening speech: 'the motto of Trinidad and Tobago says: "together we aspire, together we achieve". There could be no better description of the Commonwealth's ethos and no better guideline for achieving this CHOGM's stated goal of a more equitable and sustainable future.'

During her visit to Trinidad, local children dressed in carnival costume greeted The Queen outside the Queen's Hall in the Port of Spain. Recalling the visit in her Christmas broadcast a month later, she spoke of meeting with young people in Trinidad and Tobago, and hearing how the Commonwealth is important to them, offering practical assistance and networks to improve skills and encourage enterprise. Investing in future generations, the Queen's Young Leaders programme was set up in 2014 to support and recognise young people, aged 18–29, who are leading the way in transforming their own lives and those of others around them across the Commonwealth. During the four years of its operation, winners received a unique package of training, mentoring and networking, and were presented with their award by The Queen at Buckingham Palace.

THE DAY JOB

The Queen visits the new Elizabeth Line,
Bond Street station, London, 23 February 2016

Unveiling a commemorative plaque is a key part of the day job of any member of the Royal Family. In 2017, the 95-year-old Prince Philip even joked that he was 'the world's most experienced plaque unveiler'. During her visits to different regions of the United Kingdom, The Queen is often asked to cut a ribbon or lay a stone to mark the beginning of work on a new building, or to plant a tree in celebration of her visit. This way of making a mark on the organisations or places she visits enables The Queen to maintain visibility, which has always been a prime objective for the British monarchy.

For this visit to the new Bond Street station in 2016, The Queen matched her outfit to the lilac roundel of the Crossrail train line, a new railway for London and the south east of the country, which was renamed the 'Elizabeth Line' in 2018 in honour of the monarch. The commemorative plaque shown here was a gift from Crossrail workers. The distinctive design of the roundel has been synonymous with London's public transport system since its introduction in 1908. In 2010 Transport for London presented The Queen with her own roundel inscribed 'BUCKINGHAM PALACE'.

The Queen is not the first monarch to have had a London Underground line named after her; the Victoria line was named after her great-great-grandmother, Queen Victoria, when the line was formally opened by The Queen on 7 March 1969. She is, though, the only British monarch ever to have travelled on the London Underground, popularly known as 'the Tube'.

_____

The Queen's diary includes attending important fixtures in the performing arts calendar, and on these glittering occasions The Queen can be relied upon to sparkle. The Queen is seen here at the 1962 Royal Variety performance at the London Palladium greeting the American performers Bob Hope and Sophie Tucker in the after-show line-up – always a special moment for the entertainers. On this occasion The Queen wore the tiara presented to her grandmother, Queen Mary, by the 'Girls of Great Britain and Ireland' on the occasion of her wedding in 1893. Queen Mary in turn gave it to Princess Elizabeth, now The Queen, for her wedding to Prince Philip.

The Royal Variety show is a fundraising event that first took place in 1912, when The Queen's grandparents, King George V and Queen Mary, attended a concert to raise money for the Entertainment Artistes' Benevolent Fund (now the Royal Variety Charity). The reigning monarch has been Life-Patron of the charity since 1921, and the event, held in December, is now televised. Her Majesty has attended 35 performances since 1949 and has served as Patron since 1952.

Another important entertainment event in The Queen's year is the Royal Command Film Performance, first held in 1946 and attended by King George VI and Queen Elizabeth, Princess Elizabeth and Princess Margaret. Since then it has become an annual event that takes place in November to raise money for the Film and TV Charity (formerly known as the Cinema and Television Benevolent Fund). Over the years, Her Majesty has met many leading figures of the film world, including Marilyn Monroe and Daniel Craig, and attended special screenings of such box-office hits as *Titanic*, in 1997, and *Casino Royale*, in 2006.

The Queen attends the World Cup Final, 30 July 1966

On 30 July 1966, Wembley Stadium in London played host to the final of the FIFA World Cup. The Queen attended the game along with more than 60,000 spectators who watched the English team defeat West Germany 4–2. This photograph quickly became iconic and is still treasured by England fans, as this was England's first and, to date, only World Cup victory. The Queen is clearly delighted to be presenting the trophy to England Captain Bobby Moore. Moore later commented that climbing the steps to meet The Queen he realised that his muddy hands might soil The Queen's white gloves so he had to use the velvet lining of the royal box to wipe them clean.

The Queen often attends major sporting events, and other members of the Royal Family are patrons of a number of national sports clubs and organisations. The Duke of Cambridge has been an Aston Villa fan since his school days, and The Duchess of Cambridge is a keen sailor and sportswoman, playing tennis and hockey. Both believe that sport has the power to engage, educate and inspire and change lives for the better.

Three months after the successful Apollo 11 Moon landing on 20 July 1969, the Royal Family welcomed pioneering astronauts Mike Collins, Neil Armstrong and Edwin 'Buzz' Aldrin to Buckingham Palace. An estimated 22 million people in Britain tuned in to watch the coverage of Neil Armstrong's historic walk on the surface of the Moon, the Royal Family among them. Cementing the national joy at this celebrated feat, The Queen was one of 50 world leaders who contributed messages of goodwill that were deposited on the Moon's surface. Written on behalf of the British people, Her Majesty's message read: 'I salute the skills and courage which have brought man to the moon. May this endeavour increase the knowledge and well-being of mankind.'

The Queen is a long-standing supporter of science, technology, engineering and human endeavour. Throughout her reign, along with the Duke of Edinburgh, Her Majesty has marked key scientific milestones, particularly in the exploration of space. In 1961 they met the Russian cosmonaut Yuri Gagarin, the first human to travel in space, at Buckingham Palace, and in 2011 they gave a reception to celebrate exploration and adventure in the UK, where they met Dr Helen Sharman, the first British astronaut in space. The Queen and Prince Philip sent a message of good luck to Major Timothy Peake, as he became the first British astronaut to join the International Space Station in December 2015: 'we hope that Major Peake's work on the Space Station will serve as an inspiration to a new generation of scientists and engineers'.

Pope John Paul II meets The Queen and the Duke of Edinburgh at the Vatican, 17 October 1980

Dressed in a long black taffeta gown and veil, in line with Vatican protocol, The Queen made history in 1980 when she became the first British monarch to make an official State Visit to the Vatican City, the seat of the Roman Catholic Church, in Rome. She and the Duke of Edinburgh were received by Pope John Paul II, who welcomed the couple in his private library. Gifts were exchanged, with The Queen offering a book about Windsor Castle, specially bound by the Royal Library (seen in the foreground of this picture).

In return, Pope John Paul II made a pastoral visit to England, Scotland and Wales in 1982, the first reigning pope ever to tread on British soil. On the death of John Paul II in 2005, The Queen sent a message to the Holy See, the central governing body of the Catholic Church, remembering the work His Holiness had done to encourage 'closer ties between the Roman Catholic and Anglican churches'.

As Titular Head of the Church of England, the Sovereign holds the title 'Defender of the Faith and Supreme Governor of the Church of England'. The title of 'Defender of the Faith' was first granted to Henry VIII by Pope Leo X in 1521, and when Henry broke with the Roman Catholic Church in 1534, he was proclaimed 'supreme head on earth' of the Church of England.

The Queen recognises and celebrates religious diversity in the UK and the Commonwealth. This is reflected in her Christmas and Commonwealth Day messages, which often address the theme of inter-faith harmony and tolerance, and the leaders of all faiths and denominations are regularly invited to royal ceremonial events such as weddings and services of thanksgiving.

This lively photograph shows The Queen and Prince Philip arriving on uneven terrain on the beach at Arromanches, Normandy, flanked by veterans proudly carrying flags and regimental banners. Members of the Royal Family travelled to northern France in 1994 to attend the memorial service marking the 50th anniversary of the Second World War D-Day Landings. The momentous events of June 1944 resulted in the largest seaborne invasion in history and ultimately led to the Allied victory against Germany.

In 2019, in a speech to mark the 75th anniversary of D-Day, The Queen said: 'the wartime generation – my generation – is resilient … the heroism, courage and sacrifice of those who lost their lives will never be forgotten. It is with humility and pleasure, on behalf of the entire country – indeed the whole free world – that I say to you all, thank you.'

The Queen and Prince Philip both contributed to the war effort (page 52) and afterwards continued to support the armed forces through their patronages. At the age of 18, Princess Elizabeth joined the Auxiliary Territorial Service early in 1945, when she was registered as No. 230873 Second Subaltern Elizabeth Alexandra Mary Windsor. After five months she was promoted to Junior Commander, the equivalent of Captain. Prince Philip, then Lieutenant Philip Mountbatten, R.N., was on active service as First Lieutenant in the Royal Navy throughout the war.

The Queen meets James Bond, 27 July 2012

The Opening Ceremony of the London 2012 Olympics featured a starring role for the monarch. An audience of 62,000 people seated inside the Olympic stadium, and a billion TV viewers watching around the world, were treated to a short film in which Daniel Craig, in his most famous role as James Bond, arrived at Buckingham Palace to a welcome from corgis Monty, Willow and Holly followed by The Queen herself, dressed in a peach crystal and lace cocktail dress, who greeted Daniel Craig with the immortal words: 'Good evening, Mr Bond'. The crowds then watched in astonishment as The Queen appeared to leap from the doors of a helicopter hovering above and parachute from 500 feet into the stadium, only to appear seconds later walking calmly to her seat.

The short film, entitled *Happy and Glorious*, had been kept a closely guarded secret during the months of its preparation. Two identical dresses had been made to enable The Queen and the parachutist to wear matching outfits and create the illusion that it was the monarch

who had undertaken the dramatic stunt. This momentous contribution to the Opening Ceremony, which took place during her Diamond Jubilee year, showed Her Majesty's great sense of fun and her willingness to play a full part in significant events in the life of the nation.

———————————

The Queen and Sir David Attenborough, the broadcaster, author and naturalist, have a long-standing friendship. As Director of Programming at the BBC, Sir David produced The Queen's Christmas broadcasts between 1986 and 1991. He was knighted by The Queen in 1985 for services to television broadcasting and conservation, and was admitted to the Order of Merit (page 80) in 2005 in recognition of his contribution to the study of anthropology and natural history.

Sir David's natural history programmes have reached audiences across the globe and, in 2018, his documentary *The Queen's Green Planet* focused on The Queen's Commonwealth Canopy project, which will lead to the creation of a network of national forest parks across the 54 Commonwealth nations. The endeavour aims to conserve and enhance indigenous forests for future generations, as well as commemorating The Queen's service to the Commonwealth. In a 2016 speech, Sir David expressed his admiration for the initiative: 'we are fortunate that you are still thinking about the future and how to make this a better world'.

The Queen and Sir David have much in common, having been born 17 days apart – The Queen on 21 April and Sir David on 8 May 1926. They also share a passion for preserving the planet. When The Queen paid tribute to Sir David's tireless work to increase awareness of this cause in 2019, she said: 'your ability to communicate the beauty and vulnerability of our natural environment remains unequalled'.

———————

In April 2020, at the start of the Covid-19 pandemic, Second World War veteran Captain Tom Moore, popularly known as 'Captain Tom', embarked on one hundred laps of his garden in the run-up to his 100th birthday, completing ten laps per day with the help of a walking frame. Initially aiming to raise £1,000 for the National Health Service, he rapidly reached his target and went on to raise more than £32 million in donations. Three months later, Captain Sir Thomas Moore stood proudly before The Queen as she conferred the honour of a knighthood in a special investiture held in the Quadrangle at Windsor Castle. This socially distanced outdoor occasion was a unique event that poignantly contrasted with the large ceremonies that usually take place inside The Queen's official residences.

An investiture provides the opportunity for The Queen to honour an individual's service to the nation, whether this be in commerce, industry, science, the arts, education or charitable work. The awards allow The Queen to express her gratitude for and recognition of a contribution to national life, great or small. In the course of her reign Her Majesty has presented more than 400,000 honours and awards, and some 25 investitures take place each year, with around 300 people in attendance on each occasion.

In 2016, The Queen spoke about the importance of honouring people from all walks of life: 'to be inspirational you don't have to save lives or win medals. I often draw strength from meeting ordinary people doing extraordinary things: volunteers, carers, community organisers and good neighbours; unsung heroes whose quiet dedication makes them special.'

During the coronavirus pandemic, the Royal Family had to cancel or postpone all their public engagements in the interests of health and safety. At the age of 94, The Queen fell within the 'at-risk' category and self-isolated at Windsor Castle throughout the pandemic, accompanied by a small but dedicated team of staff fondly known as HMS *Bubble*.

Even though she was unable to meet people in person, Her Majesty worked remotely to applaud the work of charity and healthcare workers across the United Kingdom. In a televised address filmed at Windsor Castle at the beginning of the first lockdown, on 5 April 2020, The Queen thanked key workers for continuing to provide essential services, and everyone who was staying at home to prevent the spread of the virus. The famous billboard in Piccadilly Circus in central London was emblazoned with an image from the broadcast, accompanied by Her Majesty's words of hope for happier times ahead: 'we will be with our friends again; we will be with our families again; we will meet again'.

The Queen was able to maintain a busy schedule of private audiences via video call. This collage of photographs is taken from various virtual meetings held during the lockdown year. They included online meetings to celebrate Volunteers' Week, to congratulate a selection of winners of the Commonwealth Points of Light award, highlighting the importance of volunteers across the Commonwealth, and with The Princess Royal and the Carers Trust, which provides support for all those people who look after a friend or family member who is ill, frail, disabled or has mental health or addiction problems. To mark World Sight Day 2020, The Queen joined The Countess of Wessex for a video call with eye health professionals working to deliver eye care across the Commonwealth during the pandemic.

FAMILY

The Queen and family at the Royal Windsor Horse Show, 14 May 1955

On the death of her father, King George VI, in 1952, life changed dramatically for the 26-year-old Princess Elizabeth and her young family. After their marriage in 1947, the Princess and the Duke of Edinburgh divided their time between Windlesham Moor, their country residence not far from Windsor Castle, and Clarence House, part of the St James's Palace complex in London. In May 1952, the new Queen moved her family into Buckingham Palace, the administrative headquarters of the British monarchy, and still the Sovereign's official residence in London.

The Queen is seen here, three years after her accession, on a visit to the annual Royal Windsor Horse Show with Prince Philip and their children, Prince Charles (aged six) and Princess Anne (aged four). Young as she was, Princess Anne watched the proceedings attentively because her pony, William, was competing in the children's pony class, ridden by 10-year-old Juliet Horder, who was highly commended, and received a rosette from The Queen.

At a casual glance this could be any ordinary family in 1950s Britain. The Queen's new role, however, sometimes entailed long periods of separation from her children. In 1953–4, for example, she and Prince Philip undertook a six-month tour of the Commonwealth (pages 38 and 72), leaving Prince Charles and Princess Anne in the care of their grandmother, Queen Elizabeth The Queen Mother.

Speaking in 1972 to mark her Silver Wedding anniversary, The Queen said: 'if I am asked what I think about family life after 25 years of marriage, I can answer with equal simplicity and conviction, I am for it'.

The Royal Family at Frogmore House, 1968

———————————

The Queen and the Duke of Edinburgh's family was completed with the births of Prince Andrew in 1960 and Prince Edward in 1964. Speaking about the joys of motherhood after the birth of Prince Edward, The Queen said: 'all of us who have been blessed with young families know from long experience that when one's house is at its noisiest, there is often less cause for anxiety. The creaking of a ship in a heavy sea is music in the ears of the captain on the bridge.'

This portrait was taken at Frogmore House, in the Home Park on the Windsor Castle estate. Frogmore has been used as a royal retreat since 1792 when it was purchased by Queen Charlotte, wife of George III. The Queen employed the architect James Wyatt to enlarge and modernise the house in the 1790s. Passed down through the family, Frogmore has served as the setting for many happy family occasions, including the wedding receptions of several of The Queen's grandchildren and other members of her close family.

The Queen invests Prince Charles as Prince of Wales, 1 July 1969

Following his mother's Accession, Prince Charles became heir apparent to the throne and, in recognition of this, The Queen bestowed the honorary title of Prince of Wales on her eldest son in a colourful ceremony held at Caernarfon Castle in north Wales on 1 July 1969. Prior to the Investiture, Prince Charles spent a term at the University College of Wales, in Aberystwyth, learning to speak Welsh.

Having already invested Charles with a sword, The Queen here places a specially designed 24-carat gold coronet on the Prince's head, after which he was given a ring, rod and mantle. Wearing these signs of rank, the Prince then pledged his allegiance to The Queen with the words: 'I, Charles, Prince of Wales, do become your liege man of life and limb and of earthly worship and faith.'

The Queen's respect for the stability and continuity for future generations offered by the line of succession also extends to her position as Head of the Commonwealth. Although the role is not hereditary, Her Majesty declared her sincere wish that the Prince of Wales 'should carry on the important work started by my father in 1949'. The Commonwealth leaders unanimously named Prince Charles as The Queen's successor at the end of the Commonwealth Heads of Government Meeting held in 2018.

The Prince of Wales often assists The Queen in the performance of her official duties, undertaking State Visits and regional tours in her name and regularly conducting investitures. In November 2018 she gave a toast at a party to celebrate his 70th birthday, where she declared her eldest child 'a dedicated and respected heir to the throne to stand comparison with any in history – and a wonderful father'.

The Queen on holiday in Scotland, 1971

This idyllic view of The Queen in Scotland, accompanied by two of her beloved corgis, was taken beside a waterfall on the Garbh Allt burn on the Balmoral estate, during the Royal Family's annual summer holiday.

Balmoral Castle, in Aberdeenshire, has been one of the Sovereign's private residences since the estate was purchased by Queen Victoria and Prince Albert in 1852 as a place for their growing family to escape city life during the summer months. The Queen has visited Balmoral regularly since her childhood and usually spends two months there every summer with her family. In her own words: 'it is rather nice to hibernate for a bit when one leads such a movable life'.

The photograph is one of a series commissioned to mark The Queen and Prince Philip's Silver Wedding anniversary in 1972. A family portrait from this series, showing The Queen, Prince Philip and their children relaxing on the estate, was chosen as the family's Christmas card for that year. It is significant that the couple chose Balmoral as the setting for their anniversary as they had spent so much time together in Scotland: first as a newly engaged couple in July 1947 and subsequently as husband and wife, parents, grandparents and great-grandparents.

The photographer, Patrick Lichfield, who was a cousin of The Queen, said that while at Balmoral, the Royal Family 'act as normal people' and 'lunch is always outdoors and they are outside every day going on expeditions'. Her Majesty also hosts the annual Ghillies' Ball at the castle, where she takes part in traditional Scottish country dancing. Guests include estate and castle staff, and members of the local community. The first reel of the evening is usually an eightsome, and members of the Royal Family traditionally make up the first set.

During their Scottish summer holiday, the family often wear tartan. In the mid-19th century Queen Victoria and Prince Albert created their own Balmoral Tartan, which is still worn by The Queen today and also used extensively for furnishings at Balmoral Castle. It is just one of several tartans exclusive to the Sovereign's family.

The christening of Prince William, 4 August 1982

Prince William Arthur Philip Louis, the first child of The Prince and Princess of Wales, was born on 21 June 1982. The infant Prince was christened on 4 August in the Music Room at Buckingham Palace, the site of many royal christenings over the years, including that of Prince Charles in December 1948. Prince William's proud parents posed for the official portraits with The Queen, Prince Philip and the Queen Mother, who happened to be celebrating her 82nd birthday on that day.

As the first-born child of Prince Charles, Prince William is second in line to the throne. The order of succession to the throne is through descent, but it is also regulated by Parliament. Before 2014, the order favoured male heirs, so younger sons would succeed to the throne before their older sisters. The Succession to the Crown Act (2013) removed this rule, so Prince William's daughter, Princess Charlotte (born 2015), now takes precedence in the line of succession over her younger brother, Prince Louis (born 2018).

On his 21st birthday, Prince William was appointed a Counsellor of State, standing in for The Queen on official occasions and working in support of The Queen through his programme of charitable work, royal duties and engagements in the UK and overseas. He was made Duke of Cambridge after his marriage to Catherine Middleton in 2011. In 2015, the Prince spoke fondly of his grandmother's inspiring role: 'all of us who will inherit the legacy of my grandmother's reign and generation need to do all we can to celebrate and learn from her story. Speaking for myself, I am privileged to have The Queen as a model for a life of service to the public.'

The Queen attends church on Christmas Day,
25 December 2003

The Queen's much-loved Sandringham estate, in Norfolk, was purchased as a coming-of-age present for the Prince of Wales, the future King Edward VII, in 1862 and several generations of the Royal Family have since enjoyed visits to the Jacobean-style house and its 60 acres (24 hectares) of formal garden. The Queen was taken to Sandringham on a visit to her grandparents, King George V and Queen Mary, in 1926, when she was only eight months old, and she has been a frequent visitor ever since. During the 1960s, when Her Majesty's children were small, many Christmases were celebrated at Windsor Castle, but from 1988, when the castle was being rewired, the family returned to Sandringham House for the festive season, establishing the now customary Christmas and New Year family gathering.

In line with traditions established by Queen Victoria and Prince Albert, the members of the Royal Family exchange their gifts on Christmas Eve. On Christmas Day The Queen attends the morning service at the nearby church of St Mary Magdalene along with her children, grandchildren and great-grandchildren. After the service, The Queen talks to well-wishers from the community. Here, assisted by her grandchildren, the Princesses Beatrice and Eugenie, she receives flower bouquets from local children waiting outside the church.

Attending the Highland Games, 2 September 2006

The Braemar Highland Games, also known as the Braemar Gathering, is a long-standing fixture in The Queen's diary during her annual trip to Scotland. The competition is held on the first Saturday in September and is a celebration of Highland culture and sportsmanship that has taken place for around 900 years, dating back to a time when clans would compete against each other in feats of skill and strength.

The games include caber tossing, tone (knife)- and hammer-throwing, track events, traditional piping, dancing and tug-of-war. The Queen's great-great-grandmother, Queen Victoria, was the first member of the Royal Family to attend the games, in 1848, with her husband, Prince Albert, and their children, and the tradition of the attendance of the reigning monarch with their family has continued since then.

The Queen always visits with those members of the Royal Family who have joined her at the nearby Balmoral estate for a summer holiday. The Prince of Wales, who is Patron of the Scottish Highland Games Association, and his wife, The Duchess of Cornwall, joined Her Majesty and the Duke of Edinburgh in 2006, where the family group were photographed in high spirits as they watched the events with evident delight.

The christening of Prince George, 23 October 2013

Prince George was born at 4.24pm on 22 July 2013. As the first child of
The Duke and Duchess of Cambridge, he was born third in line to the
throne. His christening took place three months later at the Chapel Royal,
St James's Palace, after which the Royal Family returned to the Morning Room
at Clarence House, where this portrait was taken, officially marking the latest
addition to the direct line of succession to the throne.

Prince George wore a hand-made replica of the historic royal christening
gown that had been commissioned by Queen Victoria for the baptism of her
eldest daughter, Princess Victoria, in 1841. Made from Spitalfields silk with
a Honiton lace overlay, the original gown was inspired by the dress created
for Queen Victoria's marriage to Prince Albert in 1840 and made by Janet
Sutherland, the daughter of a coal miner from Falkirk, Scotland, who received
the title 'Embroiderer to the Queen' for her efforts.

The gown has been worn by 62 royal babies since it was created, including
Princess Elizabeth (the future Queen Elizabeth II) at her christening in the
private chapel at Buckingham Palace on 29 May 1926. Last worn in 2004,
for the christening of Lady Louise Windsor, daughter of The Earl and
Countess of Wessex, the original gown is now too fragile to be used. A copy
was then made by Angela Kelly, dressmaker to The Queen, in 2004 and
this was used for Prince George's christening.

Water from the River Jordan was used for the baptism, which was
performed by the Archbishop of Canterbury, Justin Welby. Afterwards, The
Prince of Wales and The Duchess of Cornwall gave a private tea in Clarence
House where guests were served slices of christening cake consisting of one
of the tiers saved from The Duke and Duchess of Cambridge's wedding cake.

The Queen with her grandchildren and great-grandchildren, April 2016

To mark her 90th birthday, The Queen was photographed with her two youngest grandchildren and her five great-grandchildren in the Green Drawing Room at Windsor Castle. Two other portraits were released to celebrate the occasion, one showing Her Majesty with her corgis, and the other with her only daughter, Princess Anne. Annie Leibovitz, the photographer, set out to depict The Queen not as Sovereign, but as 'Gan Gan', as she is affectionately known by her great-grandchildren. This intimate portrayal of the monarch, with her then youngest great-grandchild, Princess Charlotte, sitting on her knee, shows how much she values time spent with her family.

In her 2018 Christmas speech to the nation, The Queen joked that her growing family kept her 'well occupied'. During The Queen and Prince Philip's long marriage they welcomed four children, eight grandchildren and a growing number of great-grandchildren. In the documentary *Our Queen at 90*, which aired the same year that this photograph was taken, The Duchess of Cambridge revealed that The Queen likes to spoil her grandchildren, leaving gifts in their rooms when they come to stay, 'and that just shows her love for her family'.

MILESTONES

The Queen's walkabout after the Silver Jubilee Service
of Thanksgiving, 7 June 1977

———————

The Queen celebrated the 25th anniversary of her accession with
a Service of Thanksgiving at St Paul's Cathedral on 7 June 1977,
attended by numerous world leaders, including the British Prime
Minister, James Callaghan, and the US President, Jimmy Carter.
This was followed by a banquet hosted by the Lord Mayor of London
at the Guildhall at which Her Majesty referred to the broadcast she
had made on the occasion of her 21st birthday (page 82): 'when I was
twenty-one I pledged my life to the service of our people and I asked
for God's help to make good that vow. Although that vow was made
in my salad days, when I was green in judgement, I do not regret nor
retract one word of it.'

After the service, The Queen took one of her customary walkabouts
to meet some of the one million well-wishers who had lined the route
of the royal procession from the City of London back to Buckingham
Palace. Many more people took part in processions and street parties
across the nation.

The striking pink dress and coat chosen by The Queen for the
occasion was designed by Hardy Amies, the couturier renowned for
his impeccably elegant tailoring. This was complemented by a playfully
designed hat created by Simone Mirman, The Queen's long-time milliner,
with 25 stylised flowerheads hanging from silk threads at the back.

The Golden Jubilee parade, 4 June 2002

For her Golden Jubilee in June 2002, The Queen was greeted by vast flag-waving crowds as she and Prince Philip led a glittering parade along The Mall from Buckingham Palace and on to St Paul's Cathedral for a Service of Thanksgiving. The Queen chose to travel in the Gold State Coach for the Jubilee parade, the same coach that had taken her from Buckingham Palace to her Coronation at Westminster Abbey, 50 years earlier, on 2 June 1953. The day prior to the parade was marked by the 'Party at the Palace', a public concert opened by Queen guitarist Brian May who played the national anthem from the roof of Buckingham Palace, watched by some 200 million television viewers around the world.

The Queen hosted six Garden Parties during the spring and summer, including one with the special theme of Accession Day Babies attended by 688 people born on 6 February 1952. This was also the year that Her Majesty opened the two Queen's Galleries at Buckingham Palace and the Palace of Holyroodhouse in Edinburgh, which today host special exhibitions of works of art from the Royal Collection.

In her Golden Jubilee speech at London's Guildhall, The Queen said: 'gratitude, respect and pride: these words sum up how I feel about the people of this country and the Commonwealth – and what this Golden Jubilee means to me'. It was a year tinged with sadness, however, as her much-loved sister, Princess Margaret, Countess of Snowdon, died on 9 February 2002, and her mother, Queen Elizabeth The Queen Mother, had died seven weeks later, on 30 March 2002 (aged 101).

The Queen reads her birthday cards, April 2006

The Queen celebrated her 80th birthday at Windsor Castle on 21 April 2006. That morning she and Prince Philip spent nearly an hour on an informal walkabout, meeting some of the more than 20,000 well-wishers who had lined the streets outside Windsor Castle.

Her Majesty received some 30,000 birthday cards, many of which had been made by hand. Here she is seen reading a selection in the Regency Room at Buckingham Palace. In a personal message of thanks for the mountains of post received, she said: 'I would like to thank the many thousands of people from this country and overseas who have sent me cards and messages on my eightieth birthday. I have been very touched by what you have written, and would like to express my gratitude to you all for making this day such a special one for me.'

In a birthday speech given at a banquet in her honour held at London's Banqueting House, she showed her sense of humour by quoting Groucho Marx, who once said: 'anyone can get old – all you have to do is live long enough'. Instead, she drew attention to 'the many other anniversaries this year which are more deserving of celebration', including the 50th anniversary of the Duke of Edinburgh's Award and the 30th anniversary of The Prince's Trust, both of which had, in their different way, changed countless people's lives for the better, thanks to the 'imagination, energy and endless hard work of many dedicated people combined with the leadership and drive of The Duke of Edinburgh and The Prince of Wales'.

The Queen and the Duke of Edinburgh celebrate their Diamond Wedding anniversary, November 2007

To mark their Diamond Wedding anniversary in 2007, The Queen and the Duke of Edinburgh returned to Broadlands, the home of Prince Philip's uncle, Lord Mountbatten, where they spent their honeymoon, to re-create a photograph from their first holiday as a married couple. Faithfully copying the exact pose from the original black-and-white portrait, Her Majesty wore the same Sapphire Chrysanthemum brooch that had been given to her as an official gift when she launched an oil tanker, appropriately named the *British Princess*, in 1946.

In a speech to mark their Golden Wedding anniversary in 1997, Her Majesty spoke fondly of her consort: 'he is someone who doesn't take easily to compliments but he has, quite simply, been my strength and stay all these years, and I, and his whole family, and this and many other countries, owe him a debt greater than he would ever claim, or we shall ever know'.

Two decades later, in 2017, The Queen and the Duke of Edinburgh celebrated their Platinum wedding anniversary – the first British royal couple

to reach this milestone. Their long and happy marriage ended when His Royal Highness The Prince Philip, Duke of Edinburgh passed away peacefully at Windsor Castle on 9 April 2021.

The Queen celebrates her Diamond Jubilee, 5 June 2012

In February 2012 The Queen became only the second British monarch to celebrate 60 years on the throne, following in the footsteps of Queen Victoria (r. 1837–1901), her great-great-grandmother, who celebrated her own Diamond Jubilee in 1897. Events took place throughout the year, culminating in a weekend of celebrations in early June. One highlight of the festivities was the Thames Diamond Jubilee Pageant, on 3 June, which saw The Queen and other members of the Royal Family travel down the river in the royal barge MV *Spirit of Chartwell*, accompanied by a flotilla of 670 decorated vessels of all shapes and sizes, from rowing boats to military and commercial craft.

On 4 June a spectacular concert took place on a stage surrounding the Queen Victoria memorial in front of Buckingham Palace culminating in a performance by Sir Paul McCartney and a grand firework display. The following day The Queen made a highly anticipated appearance on the balcony of the palace, overlooking the impressive monument dedicated to her ancestor, where she watched a red, white and blue RAF flypast over The Mall.

This photograph captures a special moment on the balcony when The Queen and Prince William, a future king, share a smile as they listen to the cheers of well-wishers in The Mall. The Royal Family's appearances on the famous balcony at Buckingham Palace have formed the backdrop to some of the most memorable scenes in British history. It was Queen Victoria and Prince Albert who first stepped out onto the newly built balcony in 1851, starting a much-loved tradition that continues to this day.

The Queen becomes Britain's longest reigning monarch, 2015

On 9 September 2015, Her Majesty Queen Elizabeth II became the longest reigning monarch in British history, passing the previous record held by her great-great-grandmother, Queen Victoria, who reigned for 63 years, 7 months and 2 days. At the moment she reached this historic milestone, The Queen continued working as if it was any other day, travelling across Scotland by Royal Train to open the new Borders Railway, linking Edinburgh to Galashiels and Tweedbank.

The Queen told well-wishers that the accolade of longest reigning monarch was 'not one to which I have ever aspired'. She added, modestly, that 'inevitably, a long life can pass by many milestones; my own is no exception. But I thank you all, and the many others at home and overseas, for your touching messages of great kindness.'

Mary McCartney was commissioned to take the official photograph to mark the occasion in July 2015. The Queen chose to be photographed in her Audience Room at Buckingham Palace, working as she does every day, reading papers from her famous red box of official correspondence (page 42). She is surrounded by photographs of family members, including a portrait of her mother, Queen Elizabeth The Queen Mother. Behind her on the chair sits a familiar black handbag, an accessory that has been a firm fixture of The Queen's working wardrobe since the 1960s.

The Patron's Lunch on The Mall, 12 June 2016

The Queen celebrated her 90th birthday on 21 April 2016, while official celebrations took place across the UK and the Commonwealth in June. The Mall in St James's Park was transformed for the largest ever street party, called 'The Patron's Lunch', to celebrate Her Majesty's patronage of more than 600 charities and organisations. Around 10,000 members of the public, most of whom were chosen from the Patron's organisations, were invited to take part in a traditional British street party featuring hamper-style lunches on long tables. The event inspired many people across the United Kingdom and the Commonwealth to host their own street parties, raising funds for local initiatives and community programmes.

The typically wet British summer failed to dampen people's spirits, and members of the Royal Family joined the crowds for a walkabout down The Mall. The Queen and the Duke of Edinburgh led a promenade of vehicles along the processional route from Buckingham Palace, joined by The Duke and Duchess of Cambridge and Prince Harry in open-top cars.

The Duke of Cambridge paid tribute to his 'Granny' in her 90th year: 'my family has had plenty of reason to celebrate since The Queen turned 90 in April: The Queen's strong health and relentless energy; her sharp wit and famous sense of humour; and the fact that The Queen remains very much at the helm of our family, our nation and the Commonwealth.'

The Platinum Jubilee year

In 2022, Her Majesty The Queen will become the first British monarch to celebrate a Platinum Jubilee, marking 70 years of service since her accession in 1952. A spectacular year-long programme of events has been designed to enable people throughout the United Kingdom, the Commonwealth and the world to come together and celebrate.

The Jubilee will be an opportunity for looking forward as well as back, and when The Queen attended the G7 summit in June 2021, the floral dress she wore at an event at the Eden Project spoke volumes for her concern for the future of the planet. To honour the monarch's 70-year reign, she and Prince Charles have launched a Green Canopy campaign, urging people across the UK to 'plant a tree for the Jubilee'. Schools and community groups will be able to apply for a share of three million free saplings being provided by the Woodland Trust as part of the project. These will be planted in private gardens or in community gardens and Platinum Jubilee copses on council land or in new housing developments.

During her 70-year reign, The Queen herself has planted more than 1,500 trees around the world. In 2015, she launched The Queen's Commonwealth Canopy project (see page 102) with an appeal to Commonwealth nations to nominate areas of indigenous forest that would be preserved in perpetuity to mark Her Majesty's lifetime of service to the Commonwealth. Prince Charles said that planting trees and hedgerows was a 'statement of hope and faith in the future', and that protecting existing woodlands and forests were simple, cost-effective ways to protect the planet.

The Platinum Jubilee festivities will culminate in a Service of Thanksgiving for Her Majesty's reign at St Paul's Cathedral on Friday 3 June 2022. The following day, Buckingham Palace will form the backdrop to a live concert featuring some of the world's biggest names in entertainment in performances inspired by The Queen's seven-decade-long reign. Communities across the nation will be encouraged to host their own street parties on Sunday 5 June 2022, whilst the streets of London will witness a Platinum Jubilee Pageant featuring street arts, theatre, music, circus, carnival and costume.

ACKNOWLEDGEMENTS

We are grateful to Her Majesty The Queen for permission to produce this book and to use extracts from her various speeches, all of which are Crown copyright.

Our thanks also go to the following colleagues across the Royal Household who have helped with the compilation of this book: Lauren Briant, Florence Burnaby-Davies, Sally Goodsir, Ian Grant, Caroline de Guitaut, Lady Susan Hussey, Tim Knox, Tom Laing-Baker, Karen Lawson, Matt Magee, Alessandro Nassini, Daniel Partridge, Rachel Peat, Tori Stobie and Dee Vianna.

All images are Royal Collection Trust / © Her Majesty Queen Elizabeth II 2022 unless otherwise indicated below.

Royal Collection Trust is grateful for permission to reproduce the following:

Front cover, p. 57: Royal Collection Trust / © Her Majesty Queen Elizabeth II 2022. Photographer: David Cheskin
p. 2 © Ian Jones
pp. 5, 17, 43, 113, 132 Royal Collection Trust / All Rights Reserved
pp. 7, 21, 39, 41, 45, 47, 53, 59, 61, 63, 65, 67, 71, 81, 85, 87, 89, 99, 105, 111, 117, 121, 127, 131, 135, 139, 141, 143, back cover © PA / Alamy
p. 11 Photograph by Lisa Sheridan / Studio Lisa / Hulton Archive / Getty Images
p. 22 Stamp design used with kind permission of Royal Mail Group Limited
p. 24 © Estate of Patrick Matthews
p. 27 Photograph by Lichfield
pp. 29, 97 Photograph by Anwar Hussein / WireImage
p. 31 © Cecil Beaton / Victoria and Albert Museum, London
p. 33 © David Dawson / Bridgeman Images
pp. 35, 125 © Annie Leibovitz
p. 37 © Jayde Taylor / Twitter
p. 49 Royal Collection Trust / © Her Majesty Queen Elizabeth II 2022. Photographer: Ian Jones
p. 51 © Reuters / Chris Jackson
pp. 55, 83, 119, 133 Photograph by Tim Graham Photo Library via Getty Images

p. 69 Photograph by Jeff J Mitchell / Getty Images
pp. 75, 109 Photograph by Paul Popper / Popperfoto via Getty Images
p. 79 Photograph by Anwar Hussein / Getty Images
p. 91 Photograph by Popperfoto via Getty Images
p. 93 Photograph by Rolls Press / Popperfoto via Getty Images
p. 100 © Reuters / Jorge Silva
p. 101 © 2012 International Olympic Committee
p. 103 © ITN Productions / Shutterstock.com
p. 107 (top) © Royal Communications / PA; (bottom) © Royal Communications
p. 115 Photograph by Lichfield Archive via Getty Images
p. 123 Photograph by Jason Bell, Camera Press London
p. 129 Photograph by Sion Touhig / Getty Images
p. 137 Royal Collection Trust / All Rights Reserved. Photographer: Mary McCartney

Every effort has been made to trace and credit all known copyright or reproduction rights holders; the publishers apologise for any errors or omissions and welcome these being brought to their attention.

Published 2021 by Royal Collection Trust
York House
St James's Palace
London SW1A 1BQ

Royal Collection Trust / © Her Majesty Queen Elizabeth II 2022

Reprinted 2022

ISBN 978 1 909741 82 9

102685

British Library Cataloguing-in-Publication Data:
A catalogue record of this book is available from the British Library.

Written and edited by Polly Fellows and Kate Owen
Designed by Raymonde Watkins
Project Manager: Polly Fellows
Publisher: Kate Owen
Production Manager: Sarah Tucker
Colour reproduction by Altaimage
Typeset in Baskerville and Shango
Printed on 150gsm Claro silk
Printed and bound in Wales by Gomer Press

FRONT COVER: The Queen attending a Garden Party
at the Palace of Holyroodhouse, 3 July 2019

BACK COVER: The Queen arriving for her Coronation, 2 June 1953

TITLE PAGE: The Queen at the State Opening of Parliament,
15 November 2006. In the 70 years of her reign, The Queen has driven
in state from Buckingham Palace to the Palace of Westminster to deliver
The Queen's Speech marking the State Opening of Parliament on
65 occasions. As she travels to and from Parliament, she wears the Diamond
Diadem, made in 1820 for George IV. The same diadem features in portraits
of The Queen used on banknotes, coins and postage stamps in the
United Kingdom.

PAGE 143: The Queen enjoying the Royal Windsor Horse Show, 15 May 2009